USING WIND TURBINES
TO FIGHT CLIMATE CHANGE

by Joanna Cooke

Focus READERS

NAVIGATOR

WWW.FOCUSREADERS.COM

Focus Readers is distributed by North Star Editions:
sales@northstareditions.com | 888-417-0195

Produced for Focus Readers by Red Line Editorial.

Content Consultant: Christopher Niezrecki, PhD, Professor of Mechanical Engineering, University of Massachusetts Lowell

Photographs ©: Shutterstock Images, cover, 1, 4–5, 8–9, 10, 14–15, 17 (wind-powered electrical grid), 17 (wind turbine parts), 19, 21, 22–23, 25, 26; Lucas Oleniuk/Zuma Press/Newscom, 7; Red Line Editorial, 13; Jens Büttner/dpa/Picture Alliance/Newscom, 29

Library of Congress Cataloging-in-Publication Data
Names: Cooke, Joanna, 1975- author.
Title: Using wind turbines to fight climate change / by Joanna Cooke.
Description: Lake Elmo, MN: Focus Readers, [2023] | Series: Fighting
  climate change with science | "Navigator." | Includes index. | Audience: Grades 4-6.
Identifiers: LCCN 2021062786 (print) | LCCN 2021062787 (ebook) | ISBN
  9781637392782 (hardcover) | ISBN 9781637393307 (paperback) | ISBN
  9781637394298 (ebook pdf) | ISBN 9781637393826 (hosted ebook)
Subjects: LCSH: Wind turbines--Juvenile liteature. | Wind power--Juvenile
  literature. | Climate change mitigation--Juvenile literature.
Classification: LCC TJ828 .C66 2023 (print) | LCC TJ828 (ebook) | DDC
  621.31/2136--dc23/eng/20220317
LC record available at https://lccn.loc.gov/2021062786
LC ebook record available at https://lccn.loc.gov/2021062787

Printed in the United States of America
Mankato, MN
082022

ABOUT THE AUTHOR

Joanna Cooke writes books for young people. Her books, including *The Sequoia Lives On, Call Me Floy*, and *Fire Shapes the World,* focus on nature and the human experience. Joanna holds an MFA in creative writing and an MEd in elementary education. Prior to writing, she spent 10 years working as an environmental educator and naturalist in California's Sierra Nevada.

TABLE OF CONTENTS

CHAPTER 1

WILLIAM KAMKWAMBA

In 2001, the African nation of Malawi experienced a severe drought. People did not have water to grow food. Many farmers lost income. As a result, families often could not afford to send their children to school. Fourteen-year-old William Kamkwamba had to drop out of school. But he wanted to keep learning.

William Kamkwamba gave talks around the world after the story about his work spread.

At a library, William found a book called *Using Energy*. It showed how a wind **turbine** made electricity. William decided to try making a turbine. He searched junkyards for parts. He found a bicycle wheel, tractor fans, wires, and more. He used them to build a machine.

Wind turned the blades. The turning blades charged a generator. A generator is a machine that turns the energy of motion into electricity. This machine sent electricity to a light bulb. The bulb turned on. Now William could read at night.

William wasn't done. He designed another wind turbine. This one powered a water pump. He and his family dug a well.

William built several wind turbines for his family's farm.

They connected the well to the generator with pipes. The pump brought water to the family's fields. Now they could grow more crops. That meant the family could make more money. They also had clean water to drink.

William's story spread around the world. Many people got excited about the power of wind.

CHAPTER 2

THE CLIMATE CRISIS

For a long time, humans have used energy to survive. Thousands of years ago, people began burning wood, charcoal, and other fuels. These fuels provided heat and helped people cook.

In the 1800s, energy sources changed. The **Industrial Revolution** had begun. People burned coal to run machines.

Coal power remains a huge source of the world's energy today.

In the early 2020s, natural gas provided nearly 25 percent of the world's electricity.

By the late 1800s, scientists had also learned to create and control electricity. Some generators used moving water for energy. Others used fossil fuels. Coal, oil, and natural gas are fossil fuels. They come from long-dead plants and animals.

Many power plants burn coal. Burning coal creates heat. The heat boils water and produces steam. Fast-moving steam turns a rotor. This part powers the generator as it turns. Then the generator creates electrical energy. That electricity is sent to homes and buildings. It powers lights, heating, and air conditioning. It also powers appliances, such as refrigerators.

Burning fossil fuels creates huge amounts of energy. However, the process also releases carbon dioxide (CO_2). This greenhouse gas stays in the atmosphere for decades. Greenhouse gases trap heat from the sun. Over time, they cause Earth's temperature to rise. That leads to **climate change**.

By the 2020s, rising temperatures were affecting the whole planet. Sea ice and glaciers were melting. Ocean levels were rising. Extreme weather was getting worse. People, plants, and animals were all struggling to survive. For example, extreme weather events were causing millions of people to leave their homes.

WHO IS RESPONSIBLE?

Every country on Earth is impacted by climate change. But certain countries are more responsible for the problem. Between 1750 and 2020, the United States and Europe created approximately half of all CO_2 emissions. Meanwhile, African countries have created just 3 percent of all CO_2 emissions.

Even so, greenhouse gas emissions stayed high in the early 2020s. And energy use was still a main driver of climate change. That's because most energy still came from fossil fuels.

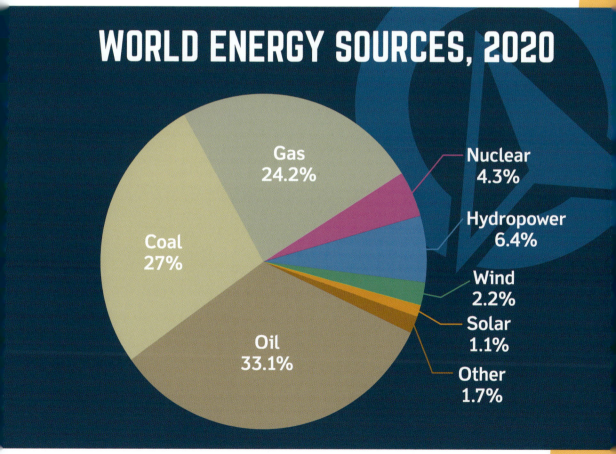

WORLD ENERGY SOURCES, 2020

- Gas 24.2%
- Nuclear 4.3%
- Hydropower 6.4%
- Coal 27%
- Wind 2.2%
- Solar 1.1%
- Other 1.7%
- Oil 33.1%

CHAPTER 3

LEANING INTO WIND

All wind has **kinetic energy**. A wind turbine changes this energy into electricity. First, wind hits the blades of a turbine. Blades usually have curved and twisted shapes. Their shapes help create **lift** from the wind. That lift causes a **torque** that rotates the blades. This gives the turbine rotating kinetic energy.

Wind turbines often have three blades. The shapes of these blades are similar to airplane wings.

The spinning blades of a turbine are called a rotor. The rotor spins a generator to make electricity. Power lines carry the electricity to an **electrical grid**. The grid sends it to where it is needed.

Other features can help turbines create more electricity. For example, winds

THE POWER OF WIND

People have used wind energy for thousands of years. Ancient Egyptians used sails to power boats. In the 900s, people built windmills in Persia. These machines used the wind to grind grain. They used the wind's kinetic energy. During the Industrial Revolution, scientists invented wind turbines. Turbines were the first machines to make electricity from wind.

become stronger higher up. So, people often build tall wind turbines. Many turbines also have wind vanes or sensors. These devices figure out which direction the wind is coming from. Then the turbine turns to face that direction.

DELIVERING WIND ENERGY

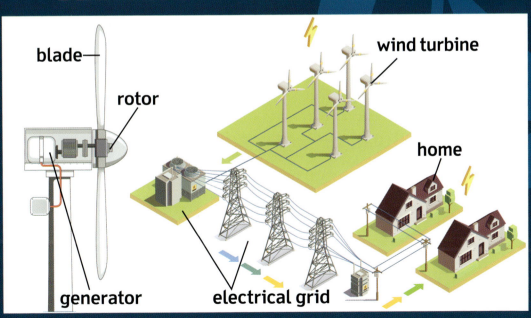

blade

rotor

wind turbine

home

generator

electrical grid

One large wind turbine can power a small town. Cities and regions use many turbines. A group of turbines is called a wind farm. Onshore wind farms are built on land. Offshore wind farms work in the ocean.

Wind turbines can help fight climate change. Most importantly, they do not release greenhouse gases into the air as they operate. Building turbines does create some emissions. That's partly because turbines are made with steel and concrete. Making these materials produces carbon emissions. Even so, wind energy still produces far fewer emissions than fossil fuels.

A worker in Russia builds part of a wind turbine's generator.

For this reason, wind turbines can help replace fossil fuels. This process is taking place across the world. In the early 2020s, countries built more wind turbines than ever before.

MINI WIND TURBINES

In 2020, the company Alpha 311 was testing a new wind turbine. The turbine would use wind made artificially by people. For example, the company planned to install turbines on the poles of streetlights. Cars push air as they drive past. This action makes wind. The company's turbines would catch that wind. Then they would power a generator.

These turbines had several advantages over regular turbines. For one, they are very quiet. Plus, they are made from recycled plastic. They are also much smaller than regular turbines. That means they can be placed nearly anywhere. The turbines are easier to install and repair as well. And they add fewer life-cycle emissions. Life-cycle

In the fall of 2020, Alpha 311 installed its first wind turbines at the O2 Arena in London, England.

emissions include all emissions from building and using turbines. New designs like this can help make wind turbines even better.

CHAPTER 4

THE PATH AHEAD

Wind energy faces several challenges. For example, people need consistent supplies of energy. However, wind strength varies. Some days might have huge, strong winds. Other days might not be windy at all. But people will still need energy on those days. This can make wind difficult to depend on.

Strong winds help wind turbines produce lots of energy.

Batteries are one solution to this problem. On windy days, turbines could store extra electricity in batteries. Then those batteries could provide power on days with little wind. However, as of 2022, batteries for wind energy were still expensive. Scientists were working on improving batteries. That would help the batteries work better. It would also make them cheaper.

Improving electrical grids is another solution. The wind might be weak at one wind farm. Meanwhile, it might be strong at another wind farm. Wind farms can share electricity. So, one farm could send power to the area with weak wind. When

Large wind farms can have hundreds of turbines. They can power hundreds of thousands of homes.

the wind shifts, power-sharing can shift, too. Better grids could make this sharing easier. That would make wind power more dependable.

When there is not enough wind, areas need a backup energy source. In the early

 Solar power and wind power can work together to provide more-reliable sources of renewable energy.

2020s, fossil fuels made up most of that backup energy. But over time, electrical grids can shift to other renewable sources. They could use solar power or hydropower. That way, greenhouse gas emissions will remain low.

Wind turbines face other challenges, too. Picking the best place for a wind farm can be tricky. Some turbines are loud. And people find others unpleasant to look at.

However, scientists have developed solutions for many of these issues. For instance, people often build wind farms far from cities. Fewer people are bothered by them there. More wind farms can also go offshore. These turbines have less impact on people and nature. Plus, wind is more constant over the ocean.

New blade designs can help, too. They make turbines quieter and more pleasant to look at. With these improvements, people may be more likely to accept wind farms near their homes.

As of 2022, many countries were leading the way with wind. For example, wind provided nearly half of Denmark's electricity needs. Uruguay was another

FLOATING WIND

Many offshore wind turbines go all the way to the seafloor. They can't be built very far from coasts. Out at sea, water is too deep. However, workers built a new kind of offshore turbine in 2020. These turbines float on the surface. Long chains anchor them. As a result, they can work in deep water miles from shore. Winds are stronger and more consistent far out at sea. For this reason, floating offshore turbines can provide steadier supplies of energy.

In 2020, workers tested floating offshore wind turbines off the coast of Germany.

leader in wind energy. Scientists keep improving the technology behind wind turbines. In many ways, the technology is ready. More governments just need to act.

FOCUS ON
USING WIND TURBINES

Write your answers on a separate piece of paper.

1. Write a sentence describing the main ideas of Chapter 4.

2. Would you want your home to be powered by wind turbines? Why or why not?

3. All wind has what type of energy?

> **A.** kinetic energy
> **B.** fossil fuel energy
> **C.** electrical energy

4. Why might improving batteries help more people use wind power?

> **A.** When there's less wind, batteries could help create more wind.
> **B.** When there's less wind, people could use energy stored in batteries.
> **C.** When there's less wind, batteries could make energy from fossil fuels.

Answer key on page 32.

GLOSSARY

climate change
A human-caused global crisis involving long-term changes in Earth's temperature and weather patterns.

electrical grid
A complex network that delivers electricity from power sources to users.

emissions
Chemicals or substances that are released into the air, especially ones that harm the environment.

Industrial Revolution
Starting in Great Britain in the 1700s, a huge economic shift involving the use of powerful machines and mass production.

kinetic energy
Energy that an object has related to its mass and motion.

lift
A force caused by wind, often causing upward movement.

torque
A twisting force that causes an object to rotate.

turbine
A rotating machine that is turned by water, steam, or air to produce power.

TO LEARN MORE

BOOKS

Cooke, Joanna K. *Energy from Wind.* Lake Elmo, MN: Focus Readers, 2022.

Hardyman, Robyn. *Wind Power.* Bridgnorth, England: Cheriton Children's Books, 2022.

Ziem, Matthew. *Wind Power: Sailboats, Windmills, and Wind Turbines.* New York: Scholastic, 2019.

NOTE TO EDUCATORS

Visit **www.focusreaders.com** to find lesson plans, activities, links, and other resources related to this title.

INDEX

Answer Key: **1.** Answers will vary; **2.** Answers will vary; **3.** A; **4.** B